Presented to:

From:

Date:

We Are
Sisters

DEE BRESTIN

We Are Sisters

DEVOTIONAL JOURNAL

HONOR **HB** BOOKS

Inspiration and Motivation for the Seasons of Life

COOK COMMUNICATIONS MINISTRIES
Colorado Springs, Colorado • Paris, Ontario
KINGSWAY COMMUNICATIONS LTD
Eastbourne, England

Honor Books® is an imprint of
Cook Communications Ministries, Colorado Springs, CO 80918
Cook Communications, Paris, Ontario
Kingsway Communications, Eastbourne, England

WE ARE SISTERS DEVOTIONAL JOURNAL
© 2006 by Dee Brestin

Cover Design: Greg Jackson, Thinkpen Design, llc
Cover Photo Credit: 2005 © JupiterImages

First Printing, 2006
Printed in Canada

1 2 3 4 5 6 7 8 9 10 Printing/Year 10 09 08 07 06

Unless otherwise noted, Scripture quotations are taken from the *Holy Bible, New
International Version*®. *NIV*®. Copyright © 1973, 1978, 1984 by International Bible
Society. Used by permission of Zondervan. All rights reserved. Scripture quota-
tions marked KJV are taken from the King James Version of the Bible (Public
Domain); quotations marked MSG are taken from *THE MESSAGE*. Copyright © by
Eugene H. Peterson 1993, 1994, 1995, 1996, 2000, 2001, 2002. Used by permission
of NavPress Publishing Group; quotations marked NKJV are taken from the New
King James Version. Copyright © 1982 by Thomas Nelson, Inc. Used by permis-
sion. All rights reserved; and quotations marked NLT are taken from the *Holy Bible,
New Living Translation,* copyright © 1996. Used by permission of Tyndale House
Publishers, Inc., Wheaton Illinois 60189. All rights reserved. Words set in plain text
in Scripture indicate emphasized text by the author.

ISBN 1-56292-724-8

*Behold, how good and how pleasant it is
for brethren to dwell together in unity!*

PSALM 133:1 NKJV

INTRODUCTION

*W*ith the release of the revised edition of *We Are Sisters,* we are also making available this personal journal for you. Even if you don't read the book, you can enjoy this journal, for scriptural principles will be repeated, but reading the book is recommended for added understanding.

Each entry includes a Scripture, brief quotations from the book, and a few reflective questions on the friendships in Scripture, or your own friendships. It is our hope this book helps you discover, as sweet as the sisterhood of women is, it pales in comparison to the power, perspective, and love we have as sisters in Christ.

In addition to reflecting on the principles in *We Are Sisters,* you will be directed to pray through a psalm each day, picking up at Psalm 60. There is a direct link between our vertical relationship with God and our horizontal relationship with people. When your relationship with God suffers, so does your relationship with people. Great men and women of God have made it a habit down through the ages to reflect and pray through the psalms. To pray a psalm, take just a few verses and make them yours. For example, in Psalm 60, David is praying concerning the enemies of Israel. It is helpful, whenever there is a prayer like this, to realize that our enemies are spiritual, for we wrestle not against flesh and blood. So, when David prays:

Give us aid against the enemy,
For the help of man is worthless.
With God we will gain the victory,
And he will trample down our enemies.

Psalm 60:11–12

You might pray something like this:

Lord, give me aid against the spiritual forces of darkness
who tell me lies. With your truth I will gain the victory
for You will set me free from my enemies.

The psalms are a rich resource for prayer. You will grow as a woman of God and, as a result, be able to give your sisters in Christ and all who cross your path more of the love, grace, and wisdom of Jesus.

When you pray Scripture, you are praying within the will of God and you will see answers. Some psalms are more difficult than others, but ask the Lord to help you find something you can understand and pray.

If you are interested in additional resources for women from Dee, check Dee's Web site (www.deebrestin.com). You can see a clip of Dee speaking, find out if Dee is speaking in your area, contact her, and find out her latest recommendations of books or movies.

A LITTLE HELP
FROM MY FRIENDS

Day One

As iron sharpens iron, so one man sharpens another.

PROVERBS 27:17

As sweet as the sisterhood of women is, it pales in comparison to the power, perspective, and love we have as sisters in Christ.

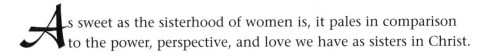 There was a time when my young marriage nearly collapsed under "hurricane winds," but my sisters in Christ helped me to survive. Can you remember a time when sisters in Christ helped you not be swallowed up by a storm? What did they do?

Women's friendships are wonderful. How can the relationship of sisters in Christ be even better?

I have just come from a gathering of women. For three hours this morning the four of us sat in a local restaurant, sharing our needs, our concerns, our unanswered questions—our hearts. Two of us cried after deep confessionals; all of us laughed.... When it was time to go—as other commitments called—we ran outside into the spring rain, lighthearted as children out for recess.

—BRENDA HUNTER

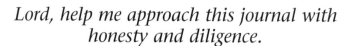

Lord, help me approach this journal with honesty and diligence.

Read, reflect, journal, and pray through Psalm 60.

Day Two

Hear my cry, O God;
listen to my prayer.
From the ends of the earth I call to you,
I call as my heart grows faint;
lead me to the rock that is higher than I.

PSALM 61:1–2

*M*y husband and I were both in tears. There didn't seem to be a way out for us. And, as people often do when they feel like cornered rabbits, we each cried out to God for help.

Can you remember times when you cried out to the Lord in desperation and He led you to the rock that is "higher than I"? List a few.

*J*n *We Are Sisters,* you will reflect on the wonderful strengths God gave you as a woman. But you will also be encouraged to consider how to use these strengths under the guidance of the Holy Spirit. Even women who don't know the Lord are blessed by one another's friendship, but *there is so much more.*

What connection do you see between the health (or lack of it) of your relationship with God and the health (or lack of it) of your relationship with others?

Lord, be with me as I walk in the strength of Your Holy Spirit.

Read, reflect, journal, and pray through Psalm 61.

Day Three

My daughter, should I not try to find a home for you,
where you will be well provided for? Is not Boaz, with whose servant girls
you have been, a kinsman of ours?

RUTH 3:1−2

*A*s women, we are matchmakers! We love romance. Intriguingly, studies show that not only do we try to give our friends a little help in getting married, we also, for the most part, help them stay married.

 If you are married, how have your sisters in Christ helped your marriage? If you are single, how have you helped your married friends be more content in their marriages?

> Women's friendships promote marital stability because they meet intimacy needs which are not met by marriage, and they help diffuse anger and other volatile emotions.
>
> —S. J. OLIKER

So much of the time I only see my side—I've got blinders on. And June will say, "You know, he's probably feeling real insecure and angry." And for the first time I'll realize there's another human being mixed up in this, instead of just me and my own passions.

—INTERVIEW BY S. J. OLIKER

*R*ather than siding with the wife against the husband, a woman is much more likely to participate in what S. J. Oliker calls "marriage work," endeavoring to strengthen her friend's marriage by helping her to see the situation from his perspective, by "framing" the husband in such a way as to "ennoble him," or by diffusing her anger with humor.

Lord, make me a peacemaker. Make me gentle and wise.

Read, reflect, journal, and pray through Psalm 62.

Day Four

Yet, O LORD, you are our Father,
We are the clay, you are the potter;
we are all the work of your hand.

ISAIAH 64:8

Even the secular world seems to have acquiesced to the realization that the differences between men and women are deep, penetrating to our DNA. As a girl, I watched Mother and her friends: hugging, confiding, laughing until tears rolled down their cheeks. It wasn't that way with Dad and his friends. They traded jokes or political opinions, but they didn't CONFIDE, didn't CONSOLE, didn't CONNECT.

Write down some of the reasons that you are thankful God made you female. If there are reasons you are not thankful to be female, tell Him about that, and ask for His perspective.

*B*efore I joined the young mothers' Bible study, I felt as if I were swimming the English Channel with two little boys on my back—and we were sinking! But the emotional support I received from my new friends was like a lifeline that not only enabled us to survive, but also enabled me to give Steve the understanding and love he so desperately needed in his grueling internship.

 Are you in a good Bible study or prayer group—one that really has you digging into God's Word? If not, pray about how that could be changed. What does the Lord impress on your heart?

> Married women who had one or more close, reciprocal friendships are significantly less depressed, more satisfied with their lives, and have higher self-esteem than those who do not have such a friendship.
>
> —C. GOODENOW, PROFESSOR,
> TUFTS UNIVERSITY
> —E. L. GAIER, PROFESSOR,
> UNIVERSITY OF NEW YORK

Lord, please help me to choose friends wisely.

Read, reflect, journal, and pray through Psalm 63.

Day Five

But when I grew up, I put away childish things.

1 CORINTHIANS 13:11 NLT

Dear Tricia,

Stay away from Jill. Jill is my best friend and you are trespassing.

Don't save Jill a seat at lunch.

Don't wait for her at her locker.

Don't give her notes in the hall.

Is this clear?

Jill is my best friend and you must find a different best friend.

Stay away!!!

Love, Kelly

While the demanding possessiveness shown in the above note is characteristic of little girls, we as women, though more subtle, can have similar feelings. Whenever we think anyone or anything can meet our deepest needs, we've made that person or that thing an idol. We cling to them too tightly, we demand too much, and we are angry with anyone or anything that threatens our access to that idol.

What or whom do you think can meet your deepest needs? Be honest, for that is the first step in turning from false gods, from "broken cisterns" that cannot hold water.

My people have committed two sins:
They have forsaken me,
the spring of living water,
and have dug their own cisterns,
broken cisterns that cannot hold water.

Jeremiah 2:13

Father, make me thirsty for You, the Living Water.

Read, reflect, journal, and pray through Psalm 64.

How is it between us, Lord?

How is it between me and my sisters (or brothers)?

The Way We Were

Day One

> *Your hands made me and formed me;*
> *give me understanding to learn your commands.*

PSALM 119:73

*R*eflecting on the way we were as children also gives us insight into the nature of adult feminine friendship.

How important was it to you, as a girl, to have a good friend? What evidence do you see for your drive to connect?

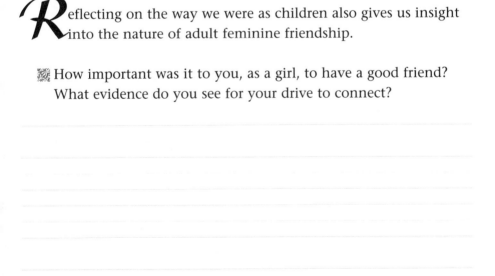

J would usually awaken first, pull on my shorts, and tiptoe barefoot over the rocky path to Barbara's cottage. I'd tap, tap, tap on her bedroom window until her familiar grin would appear through the glass. Then we'd be off to eat breakfast in our secret circle of birch trees: raspberries we'd picked ourselves and Sugar Crisp, eaten with milk in its own miniature wax-paper-lined box.

Our games were rarely competitive; they were relational. We blew bubbles in the sun, choreographed water ballets, and made a jewelry store on the beach with an inventory of shells and seagull feathers. When we talked, we connected. We'd affirm each other's bubbles, ballets, or bright designs. We told secrets and drew one another out in conversation. All this was a foreshadowing of what was to come, for as women we are still affirmers and confiders, relishing the joy of connection.

What is positive about the drive for connection?

Thank You, Lord, that You made me relational.

Read, reflect, journal, and pray through Psalm 65.

Day Two

> *The heart is deceitful above all things and beyond cure.*
> *Who can understand it?*
>
> Jeremiah 17:9

Just as some of my most cherished childhood memories are connected to Barbara, so are some of my most miserable. When little girls disagree, they know where the other is vulnerable, because they have told each other their secrets.

How have you hurt people, as a little girl or a woman, by knowing where they are vulnerable? Let God's light search you.

*W*hen Barbara and I would exchange hurtful words, we would then withdraw from one another. Our separations made us miserable. Being deprived of our friendship seemed a greater deprivation than going without food or water.

 What evidence (or the lack of it) do you see in your life that you cherish your friends but cling only to Jesus?

I dare not trust the sweetest frame
But wholly lean on Jesus' name.
—"THE SOLID ROCK"

Cleanse me, Lord. Help me to seek good,
to encourage, and to build up.

Read, reflect, journal, and pray through Psalm 66.

Day Three

> Clothe yourselves with humility toward one another, because,
> "God opposes the proud but gives grace to the humble."
>
> 1 PETER 5:5

*M*y childhood friend Barbara has not yet embraced Christ—yet she is one of the warmest women I know. We can be guilty of a snobbery that leads us to believe that only Christians can have wonderful qualities.

The book of Romans tells us that God writes His law on the hearts of believers and unbelievers. Though many have seared their consciences, others have not. What evidence do you see for morality and social conscience in some of the people you know who may not have embraced Christ?

Christians are not the only
people who have benefited
or reformed society. We
evangelicals do have a very
naive view.... Morality and
social conscience are not
limited to Christian people.

—JOHN STOTT

*Lord, forgive me for not seeing the beauty in others.
Help me to do so.*

Read, reflect, journal, and pray through Psalm 67.

Day Four

Always giving thanks to God the Father for everything,
in the name of our Lord Jesus Christ.

EPHESIANS 5:20

*B*arbara and I share something that neither of us can ever again share with someone else: childhood. I feel for Barbara a special love that many women, I have discovered, feel for a sibling or a friend with whom they shared a significant part of their childhood. Though they may be vastly different as adults, their childhood memories give them a permanent place in the other's heart.

Do you have childhood friends or siblings who have a permanent place in your heart? What memories connect you for which you could give thanks?

*W*hen I am reunited with Barbara, I am reminded of the girl in me. When I am with her, I feel younger, more carefree, and less reserved.

 List some ways you can reach out and reconnect with child-hood friends.

*Thank You, Lord, for the friends You've blessed
me with throughout life.*

Read, reflect, journal, and pray through Psalm 68.

Day Five

For we are to God the aroma of Christ among those who are being saved
and those who are perishing. To the one we are the smell of death;
to the other, the fragrance of life.

2 CORINTHIANS 2:15–16

*B*arbara and I have surmounted differences in geography, in
marital status, and in views of God. The last difference—and
I'm sure Barbara would agree—has been the most difficult.

🌸 Why might it take a lot of love for an unbeliever not to reject
you? How might you, if God permits you, love an unbeliever
in your life into the kingdom? Be specific.

*W*e no longer talk as children; we discuss the mysteries of life. I ask her questions about Jesus until she tells me she doesn't want to talk about "religion" anymore. Tears fill my eyes at the thought that she might not be in heaven with me but may, instead, face the wrath of God without a Savior. I protest that this isn't "religion" but "a relationship with Jesus Christ." Barbara casts me a warning look and I am silenced, fearful of pushing her away from the One I want her so desperately to know.

Recall some of the best experiences you shared with your favorite childhood friend and write them here. If you've lost touch with that special person, consider renewing your acquaintance.

*T*here is a theory of memory that says you remember more things when you were happy than when you were not.

Pray for the unbelievers, by name, that the Lord has in your life.

Read, reflect, journal, and pray through Psalm 69.

How is it between us, Lord?

How is it between me and my sisters (or brothers)?

NEVER UNDERESTIMATE THE POWER OF A MOTHER

Day One

I have stilled and quieted myself,
just as a small child is quiet with its mother.
Yes, like a small child is my soul within me.

PSALM 131:2 NLT

*M*others equip their daughters—positively or negatively—for future relationships.

If you had a nurturing mother, write down a few ways she particularly ministered to you. If you didn't have such a mother, was there another woman who stood in the gap? How?

*W*omen who've been blessed with a nurturing mother are likely to have rewarding friendships all of their lives. Daughters who had a cold mother or a mother who related poorly to friends herself have a harder climb ahead of them.

🖾 Do you struggle with friendships? Did your mother have trouble nurturing? Did her mother? If so, would you pray about finding good Christian counseling so that the chain can be broken?

Lord, give me insight into any generational sins that need to be broken through Your power.

Read, reflect, journal, and pray through Psalm 70.

By the time Caroline was a year and a half old ... we had an elaborate lovers' ritual to follow. When she was ready for bed, in double diapers and pajamas, I'd ask her: Do you want some mama nurse? She'd nod or say yes and ... literally run, to the rocking chair.... Within two minutes total contentment would absorb her and those blue-gray eyes would close. Calling it a lovers' ritual is not an exaggeration: I was her first love, and the depth and completeness of my response to her taught her about the possibilities of love for the rest of her life.

—Connie Marshner, *Can Motherhood Survive?*

Day Two

> *But when she could no longer hide him, she got a little basket*
> *made of papyrus reeds and waterproofed it with tar and pitch. She put*
> *the baby in the basket and laid it among the reeds along the edge*
> *of the Nile River. The baby's sister then stood at a distance,*
> *watching to see what would happen to him.*
>
> EXODUS 2:3–4 NLT

Jochebed, determined to choose life for Moses, taught Miriam crucial skills in nurturing, skills that would open up possibilities of love to her for the rest of her life. Miriam grew up to be a female prophetess, a leader of women.

How would you have kept a baby quiet when soldiers were on the prowl to murder him? Describe what you think Jochebed, the mother of Moses, went through. What impact do you think this had on Miriam?

She holds Moses one last time, feeling the velvet softness of his face in her neck, and her heart hurts. She puts him in the basket and covers him carefully. She hitches up her skirt in her waistband, picks up that basket on her hip, and steps into the reeds while Miriam, with pounding heart, watches. Then Jochebed comes back on shore and faces a little girl saying: "Remember everything we practiced, honey ... I love you so. Don't be afraid Miriam, God is with you." ... And then she does the hardest thing in her life. She walks away from her two vulnerable children and leaves them in God's hands.

—JENNIE DIMKOFF

 Place your children, grandchildren, and worries in life "in the basket" and leave them in God's hands. What are you putting in your "basket"?

Help me cast my cares on You, Lord,
and leave them there.

Read, reflect, journal, and pray through Psalm 71.

Day Three

Like mother, like daughter.

EZEKIEL 16:44

*T*he sins of the mothers, like the sins of the fathers, can be passed on from generation to generation.

 What are some ways you are glad you are like your mother? What are some ways you pray for Christ to "break the chain"?

A daughter is a mother's gender partner, her closest ally in the family confederacy, an extension of her self. And mothers are their daughters' role model, their biological and emotional road map, the arbiter of all their relationships.

—VICTORIA SECUNDA

*W*hy was Lee Ezell able to become such a loving and nurturing woman when she hadn't had a nurturing mother? It was because a sister in Christ, "Mom Croft," took the role that her own mother, for whatever reason, failed to take.

Is there a young woman in your life who needs mother love? If so, what might you do?

Then they can train the younger women to love
their husbands and children.

TITUS 2:4

Make me alert to younger women in my path, Lord.

Read, reflect, journal, and pray through Psalm 72.

Day Four

As a mother comforts her child, so will I comfort you.

ISAIAH 66:13

Experts say that our basic sense of feeling connected or sepa-rated from others is rooted in our experience as infants with our mothers. The two most common responses to having a mother who lacks "mother love" are withdrawal and dependency.

> Withdrawal is a natural response to pain. It is supernatural to instead seek out "the blessing" from God or from healthy members of the body of Christ. Why might this be wise, not only for the individual, but for the next generation?

Can a mother forget the baby at her breast
and have no compassion on the child she has borne?
Though she may forget,
I will not forget you!

ISAIAH 49:15

*S*ix-year-old Sarena had been praying for Anne, nightly, ever since she'd learned that we would be adopting a little girl. When Sarena met Anne, Anne was withdrawn and unwilling to play. Sarena looked at me and said, "Mrs. Brestin, I don't care how long it takes. I'm going to just keep on being nice to Anne, and one day we're going to be best friends."

God used Sarena, along with others, to restore Anne. Anne has discovered that she can trust others. But it took time and the kind of love that doesn't give up, like that of the Lord!

 Why is it hard to love those who have been hurt? What truths from God's Word can encourage you to continue loving?

Love never gives up.

1 CORINTHIANS 13:7 NLT

May I love with Your faithfulness, Lord.

Read, reflect, journal, and pray through Psalm 73.

Day Five

And when you find a friend, don't outwear your welcome;
show up at all hours and he'll soon get fed up.

PROVERBS 25:17 MSG

common response to a cold mother is longing for a woman to love you, sometimes to the precipice of homosexuality, but more often it is expressed in dependency. These women envelop their friends, driving them away with their neediness.

 Do you feel angry or depressed when your friend withdraws slightly or spends time with another friend? Examine your friendships.

My mother stopped showing me affection when I reached the age of five, telling me I was "too old for that." ... I always wished that I could stay a little girl so that I wouldn't lose her love. Today, as a woman, I have no interest in guys, marriage, or sex—just a desperate yearning to be loved, to be embraced, to be cherished—by an older woman.

—ANONYMOUS LETTER

*M*y friend Shannon was smothering me. What Shannon needed was Christian counseling and a friend who would put some boundaries on the friendship. God might have used me to bring healing to Shannon. Instead, I fled—wounding her again.

 Do you have a friend who smothers you? How might you respond in a helpful way to her?

Men, why are you doing this? We too are only men, human like you. We are bringing you good news, telling you to turn from these worthless things to the living God, who made heaven and earth and sea and everything in them.

ACTS 14:15

Help me worship only You, Lord.

Read, reflect, journal, and pray through Psalm 74.

How is it between us, Lord?

How is it between me and my sisters (or brothers)?

RAISING OUR CHILDREN TOGETHER

Day One

> *Two are better than one,*
> *because they have a good return for their work:*
> *If one falls down,*
> *his friend can help him up.*
> *But pity the man who falls*
> *and has no one to help him up!*
>
> ECCLESIASTES 4:9–10

Here I was—a Christian writer and speaker—but I couldn't control my own son. I didn't want to tell my friends that we had a prodigal. I tried to fix the situation myself, hoping to keep it a secret.

🔲 What are some secrets you have kept from your closest friends because of pride?

_____

_____

_____

God opposes the proud
but gives grace to the humble.

JAMES 4:6

*C*hange always begins with humility. We must take off our masks and stop praying for Aunt Jane's arthritis in prayer group and start praying for our own crippling joints: our selfishness, our gluttony, our judgmental tongues, and our failure to parent well.

🔲 Do you have a trustworthy friend with whom you can be truly honest in your battle against sin or your challenge to parent wisely? In what areas do you genuinely need prayer? Who could you trust and ask to pray with you?

Therefore confess your sins to each other and pray for each other so that you may be healed. The prayer of a righteous man is powerful and effective.

JAMES 5:16

Lord, help me to be humble and honest with my sisters.

Read, reflect, journal, and pray through Psalm 75.

Day Two

A friend loves at all times,
and a brother is born for adversity.

PROVERBS 17:17

I had *no* idea how to deal with a prodigal. Once I humbled myself, I began to seek out mentors, godly women who had successfully raised children who loved the Lord as adults.

Think of an area in which you struggle. Who do you know who has succeeded in this area and who might offer help?

*M*y mentor, Shirley, counseled me: Now is the time to love him, Dee. Rules are important, and you've set those up—but relationship is the bull's-eye.

🌀 If you are a mother, how is your relationship with each of your children? If you are not a mother, assess your relationship with others whom you desire to influence. Pray for them by name, asking God to give you love and wisdom for them.

Read, reflect, journal, and pray through Psalm 76.

Day Three

> *And Jonathan made a covenant with David*
> *because he loved him as himself.*
>
> 1 SAMUEL 18:3

*R*esearch has shown that boys are influenced profoundly by their heroes. Because status is a primary drive for boys, they want to be like the people whom they admire. Jonathan admired David for taking on the giant who was defaming God's name.

If you are a mother or a mentor to boys, how might you pray wisely for them? How might you increase their contact with godly men?

If you are married, knowing what you do about how males are influenced, how could you pray for your husband? If you are single, how could you pray for the adult males in your life? Write your prayers here.

Lord, show me how to pray powerfully and effectively for the men in my life.

Read, reflect, journal, and pray through Psalm 77.

Day Four

And Ruth said, Intreat me not to leave thee,
or to return from following after thee:
for whither thou goest, I will go;
and where thou lodgest, I will lodge:
thy people shall be my people,
and thy God my God.

RUTH 1:16 KJV

hile girls are influenced by "heroes" to a degree, research shows they are more profoundly influenced by their best friends. For their primary drive is not for status, but for connection.

If you are a mother or a mentor to girls, how might you pray wisely for them? Do so here.

What are some of the ways you remember "connecting" as a girl? How might you, as a woman, keep the beautiful part of that but let go of the unhealthy part?

"We must join hands—so," said Anne gravely. "It ought to be over running water. We'll just imagine this path is running water. I'll repeat the oath first. 'I solemnly swear to be faithful to my bosom friend, Diana Barry, as long as the sun and moon shall endure.' Now you say it and put my name in."

—Lucy Maud Montgomery, *Anne of Green Gables*

Lord, help me to cherish my friends but not cling to them. Help me to both model and teach this to the next generation.

Read, reflect, journal, and pray through Psalm 78.

Day Five

*Make level paths for your feet, so that the lame may
not be disabled, but rather healed.*

HEBREWS 12:13

*I*f we do not train our children how to get along with others,
their lame limbs may be disabled for life.

Did you have godly parents or mentors who trained you to
respond in a godly way to others when you were younger?
What did they do? If not, how has God helped you to grow
in this area?

_____

_____

_____

_____

_____

_____

_____

_____

_____

_____

_____

_____

_____

_____

_____

_____

_____

Take them by the hand and lead them in the way of the Master.

EPHESIANS 6:4 MSG

*A*fter Sally experienced unkindness from another girl, named Sue, Sally and I prayed about it, and the Scripture that came to my mind was "Do not be overcome by evil, but overcome evil with good" (Romans 12:21). Sally and I role-played different ways she could apply this verse with Sue.

Training implies actually showing someone what to do, walking him or her through an imaginary scenario. Think of children in your life who might be facing some relationship challenges. Imagine "training" them to be friendly to someone new, or kind to someone who is unkind, or how to respond to anger with a soft word. Choose a scenario, real or imagined, and write down the plan.

Lord, make me aware of young girls in my life, and help me not to miss loving them, teaching them, and praying for them.

Read, reflect, journal, and pray through Psalm 79.

How is it between us, Lord?

How is it between me and my sisters (or brothers)?

THE SIBLING BOND

Day One

> *How wonderful, how beautiful,*
> *when brothers and sisters get along!*

PSALM 133:1 MSG

*S*iblings have ties friends cannot have—the same blood runs through our veins, the same parents raised us, and the same childhood homes surrounded us.

If you have siblings, list some of the bonds you have that you do not have with friends.

After all this time—you girls still don't realize. Daddy's gone.
One day I'll be gone. Children will leave you. So will
husbands and lovers. You're the only ones who know each
other from cradle to grave.

—ELIZABETH HOFFMAN, *SISTERS*

 Comment on the above quote. Do you think you realize how
important your siblings are? What are some reasons you
should nurture the bond and try to be at peace with them?

Father, give me wisdom and love for my siblings.
Help us to dwell together in unity.

Read, reflect, journal, and pray through Psalm 80.

Day Two

When I was a child, I talked like a child, I thought like a child, I reasoned like a child. When I became a man, I put childish ways behind me.

I Corinthians 13:11

*I*f biological or adopted sisters are not close, they long to be. In order for that to happen, patterns of childhood need to be overcome, or those patterns will be like a barbed-wire fence preventing access into a beautiful garden of friendship.

What was your position in the family? How might that have established a pattern for you? Now that you are an adult, how might the Lord be asking to you to put the pattern aside?

*T*he baby in the family may expect to be the center of attention, to do little work, and to get away with it!

 If you are an older sibling, do you treat your younger siblings with the respect that adults long for? If you are a younger sibling, do you carry your share of the load in caring for aging parents, putting together family reunions, or doing dishes at Thanksgiving?

Dominating younger siblings gives older siblings an illusion of power in an unfree world.

—ELIZABETH FISHEL

Lord, help me treat my siblings the way
I long to be treated.

Read, reflect, journal, and pray through Psalm 81.

Day Three

*Now his heart yearned for his brother; so Joseph made haste
and sought somewhere to weep.*

GENESIS 43:30 NKJV

Our relationship as sisters may very well be the longest relationship of our lives; we yearn for it to be the best it can be.

How might you nurture your relationship with your sister (or sisters in Christ) today?

Journal some of your happy shared memories with your sister (or brother). If you are an only child, then do so with a close childhood friend.

> The desire to be and have a sister is a primitive and profound one ... It is a desire to know and be known by someone who shares blood and body, history and dreams.
>
> —Elizabeth Fishel

Lord, help me to love my siblings well.

Read, reflect, journal, and pray through Psalm 82.

Day Four

So Abram said to Lot, "Let's not have any quarreling between you and me,
or between your herdsmen and mine, for we are brothers."

GENESIS 13:8

*W*hen my sisters and I fought as children, our dad would sit down and give us a complex mathematical theory that siblings shared more blood than any other relation—more, even, than parent and child. Then he would lean back in his chair, smile, and say, "So let's not have any more quarreling among you—for you are sisters."

List all the reasons you can think of why you should, so far as it depends on you, be at peace with your siblings.

If your relationship with anyone is broken, strained, or even questionable, take the initiative to be reconciled. Assume that any fault is yours and be eager to confess it ... As part of diligent self-examination, ask the Lord to search you for broken relationships.

—GREG SCHARF,
PROFESSOR OF PREACHING, TRINITY EVANGELICAL SEMINARY

Be still and allow God to search you in regard to your family relationships. Wait on Him—then do whatever He tells you.

Read, reflect, journal, and pray through Psalm 83.

Day Five

Rejoice with those who rejoice,
and weep with those who weep.

ROMANS 12:15 NKJV

*B*ecause siblings have more years together than any other relatives, they are bound to share sorrow—for life is full of sorrow.

What sorrows have your siblings (or sisters in Christ) borne with you? How have they brought comfort?

*W*hen Mother died, my sisters and I held each other and wept. Feeling the enormous void, Bonnie looked at Sally and me and said, "We still have each other." And we do.

In what ways can you be a support, along with your siblings, to your aging parents? If you and your siblings have shared a sorrow together, what did you learn?

Father, help me not to look just on my own interests but on the interests of others. Give me Your heart, O Lord.

Read, reflect, journal, and pray through Psalm 84.

How is it between us, Lord?

How is it between me and my sisters (or brothers)?

CAN YOU EVER OUTGROW SIBLING RIVALRY?

Day One

> *Now Israel loved Joseph more than any of his other sons,*
> *because he had been born to him in his old age;*
> *and he made a richly ornamented robe for him.*

> GENESIS 37:3

*R*ivalry, in the Latin, means "having rights to the same stream." For siblings, that stream is the parents' love and approval.

If you are a mother, do you play favorites? What is the damage to each child when you do?

_____

_____

_____

_____

_____

_____

_____

*E*xperts say that failure to overcome rivalry separates siblings more than any factor.

 Did your parents show favoritism? If so, how could this insight help you overcome some of the walls between you and your siblings?

Parents who continually overvalue one child provide the fuel for long-lasting sibling rivalry, even, "reaching back from the grave."

—STEPHEN BOND

Father, I pray that the irritating sand of rivalry among my children may bring forth a pearl.

Read, reflect, journal, and pray through Psalm 85.

Day Two

To show partiality is not good.

PROVERBS 28:21

*M*ost children are favored for a temporary period, and that is not necessarily wrong. A wise parent keeps communicating that this perceived favoritism is temporary, and keeps showering love on the child who is hurting.

 What are some times when a child might be favored for a temporary period? How might a parent handle this wisely?

When my sister was born, it was like losing the Garden of Eden.

—ADRIANNE RICH

*J*f you grew up in a family where parents played favorites, your challenge is greater—but not insurmountable.

 List the ways God has been a Father to you, blessing you and cherishing you.

My brother Ben was born in the middle of the night. After four girls, Dad was euphoric. He ran up the stairs to our big second-story bedroom, waking us with his shout: "It's a boy! It's a boy! And Benjamin means SON OF MY RIGHT HAND!" But we felt joy, for each of us felt loved and cherished in our own right.

—CAROL KENT

Lord, help me long only for Your approval.

Read, reflect, journal, and pray through Psalm 86.

Day Three

"Bless me—me also, O my father!"
And Esau lifted up his voice and wept.

GENESIS 27:38 NKJV

Some will try to break down the door to their parents' hearts to receive this missed blessing, but all too often their attempt fails. For whatever reason, they have to face the fact that their blessing will have to come from another source.

—JOHN TRENT AND GARY SMALLEY

Did your parents give you "the blessing"? If so, how? If not, how are you dealing with it?

Are there believers in your life who you sense are hurting because they never received the parental blessing? How might you stand in the gap for them? Be still, and then write down anything the Lord impresses on your heart.

A word aptly spoken is like apples of gold in settings of silver.

PROVERBS 25:11

Lord, anoint my tongue with wisdom and my heart with bold compassion.

Read, reflect, journal, and pray through Psalm 87.

Day Four

Therefore confess your sins to each other and pray
for each other so that you may be healed.

JAMES 5:16

For years I denied that I ever competed with Ann. But today I
ashamedly admit that the feelings are there. In reality, if
women were honest, all would confess to it.... I don't think we
ever get rid of the struggle and pain of unhealthy competing.
... Rather I think our freedom comes when we can confess it.

—JAN KIEMEL ANDERSON

Ask God to search your heart and write down any feelings of
competition that you have with your siblings, or, if you are
an only child, with your sisters in Christ.

Write down a confession of rivalry. Ask God, if it is spoken in love, to bring genuine healing, or, if it has anything impure in it, to cleanse it.

Search me, O God, and know my heart;
test me and know my anxious thoughts.
See if there is any offensive way in me,
and lead me in the way everlasting.

PSALM 139:23–24

Read, reflect, journal, and pray through Psalm 88.

Day Five

Remember what the LORD your God did to
Miriam along the way after you came out of Egypt.

DEUTERONOMY 24:9

*M*iriam was gifted and used of God greatly. But after she was jealous of Moses, God punished her. Though she was forgiven, she faded out of the pages of Scripture. How much better if we confess our sin, and then, instead of looking for the blessing of man, look for the blessing of God!

Do you seek the face of God when you awake, as you go through the day, and as you go to sleep? Why is it important to do so?

*G*alatians 6:1 tells us, "If someone is caught in a sin, you who are spiritual should restore him gently." How can you confront gently? By helping her discover how this sin will hurt her.

Overcome evil with good by writing down a blessing and planning to share it with any sisters with whom you have felt rivalry.

Eric Liddell, the hero of *Chariots of Fire*, said that he ran because God made him fast, and he felt God's pleasure when he ran. When we feel the intimate pleasure of God, it doesn't matter how He chooses to work with our brothers and sisters.

—KAREN MAINS

Lord, help me draw near to You and to feel Your pleasure in me.

Read, reflect, journal, and pray through Psalm 89.

How is it between us, Lord?

How is it between me and my sisters (or brothers)?

THE TRIANGLE

Day One

Anger is cruel and fury overwhelming, but who can stand before jealousy?

PROVERBS 27:4

Two little girls play quite well together, but with three, they go for the jugular.

Did you experience the pain of the triangle in childhood? What do you remember?

If you are a mother or mentor to young girls, what are some ways that you might help them begin to find their security in God instead of their best friend?

I don't want to play in
    your yard,
I don't like you
    anymore.
You'll be sorry when
    you see me
Sliding down our
    cellar door.
You can't holler down
    our rain barrel,
You can't climb our
    apple tree,
I don't want to play in
    your yard,
If you won't be good
    to me.

—LYRICS BY PHILIP WINGATE

Father, help me train the next generation to love
You and to love one another.

Read, reflect, journal, and pray through Psalm 90.

Day Two

Treat the foreigner the same as a native. Love him like one of your own.
Remember that you were once foreigners in Egypt. I am GOD, your God.

LEVITICUS 19:34 MSG

Growing up, I was never the new kid on the block, so I wasn't particularly sympathetic to her plight.

Have you ever moved to a new town? What were some of your feelings?

How could you reach out to "the foreigner," whether it is a lonely international student, the new woman in your Bible study, or the neighbor who has just moved in? What might you do?

Lord, please help me not to be so self-absorbed that I can't see the lonely people in my life. Help me treat "the foreigner" the same as "the native."

Read, reflect, journal, and pray through Psalm 91.

Day Three

Share with God's people who are in need. Practice hospitality.

ROMANS 12:13

When we moved to Seattle I was so lonely. When they asked for prayer requests at the Bible study I visited, I started crying. I was so embarrassed to be crying in front of a group of strangers. But I'll never forget how those women responded. They hugged me, prayed for me, and started inviting me over for coffee or a walk around Green Lake.

Think about those in the past who ministered to you through hospitality. What positive memory comes to mind?

How could you draw a circle that would take in the widow, the single mother, or the unbeliever in your midst?

He drew a circle that
   shut me out,
Heretic, rebel, a thing
   to flout.
But Love and I had the
   wit to win,
We drew a circle that
   took him in.
                —EDWARD MARKHAM

Lord, help me see people as Jesus does.

Read, reflect, journal, and pray through Psalm 92.

Day Four

A person standing alone can be attacked and defeated,
but two can stand back-to-back and conquer. Three are even better,
for a triple-braided cord is not easily broken.

ECCLESIASTES 4:12 NLT

Ann told me that her very best friend from the past was moving from Florida to Fargo! Sylvia and Ann would be as snug as bugs in a rug—and I would be outside, shivering in the bitter Fargo winter!

🔖 Have you experienced the pain of a friendship triangle as a woman?

🔖 What do you think is God's perspective?

J would like to tell you that when I became a woman I put away childish ways—but I was in my thirties before I clearly saw the sin in territorial friendships.

What is the sin in territorial friendships?

Lord, help me worship You and You alone and to cherish my friends but also to hold them loosely.

Read, reflect, journal, and pray through Psalm 93.

Day Five

It is better to take refuge in the LORD than to trust in man.

PSALM 118:8

*R*ather than behaving like little girls, guarded and territorial concerning their best friend, Ann and Sylvia opened their circle, because their trust was in God rather than each other.

Are your friendships open—or guarded and territorial? Examine them.

*A*nn and Sylvia were convinced that God was leading the three of us to be friends. And when we got together, we helped each other find strength, not in each other, but in God.

 How might you and your friends do a better job of helping each other?

 Find strength in God?

Lord, fill my heart with Your love and wisdom
so it overflows to others.

Read, reflect, journal, and pray through Psalm 94.

How is it between us, Lord?

How is it between me and my sisters (or brothers)?

HUSBANDS VERSUS BEST FRIENDS

Day One

So God created man in his own image, in the image of God created he him;
male and female created he them.

GENESIS 1:27 KJV

*S*cience and Scripture agree—male and female are designed dramatically differently, right down to their DNA.

What are some differences you have noticed, generally speaking, in the way men and women communicate, connect, and console?

One day, after a particularly bitter fight, Rosalie is convinced she has lost Susan. Grieving, she says to her husband: "What will I do without a best friend?"

He says: "But you've got me!"

Rosalie shakes her head and stares out into the distance. "It's not the same."

—BEACHES

What are some ways your women friends can minister to you that most men probably could not?

Lord, thank you that You made both male and female.

Read, reflect, journal, and pray through Psalm 95.

Day Two

The eye cannot say to the hand, "I don't need you!"
And the head cannot say to the feet, "I don't need you!"

1 CORINTHIANS 12:21

Just as the hand needs the eye, it needs the other hand.

—JANE TITTERINGTON

It is important to be thankful for both men and women in our lives, for they contribute in different ways. What are some reasons you are thankful for your husband or for important men in your life?

*J*n *Just Friends*, Lillian Rubin interviewed husbands about their wives' friendships and found that many were mystified, particularly by the intensity of the friendship in the beginning. The aura of romance can seem threatening to the exclusivity of the marriage relationship. One man said:

> She thinks I don't like her friend Peg, but that's not it. (Uncomfortably) I guess maybe I'm jealous. When they first met, you'd think they were having some kind of love affair the way they were always trying to figure ways to get together and talking on the phone all the time. Why would I feel good about that?

If you are married, consider, are you putting your husband above your women friends? Or does he have a reason to feel neglected?

Lord, help me keep You first, and to honor my husband above other relationships.

Read, reflect, journal, and pray through Psalm 96.

Day Three

Husbands, likewise, dwell with them with understanding,
giving honor to the wife.

1 PETER 3:7 NKJV

*M*any men wonder, since they are content to have their only close friend be their spouse, why it can't be the same for women.

A wise woman can help her husband dwell with her with understanding. How might you help a man understand why you need both women and him in your life?

Can you think of a word picture that might tap into your husband's right brain and turn the light on, helping him understand your need for women friends?

> I told Mike I have this fountain of words bubbling up from my heart, and if I used them all on him he might drown! He laughed, and I think he really does understand and is very supportive of my need to be with other women.
>
> —JOAN,
> A WOMAN FROM NEW JERSEY

Lord, help me help my husband dwell with me with understanding.

Read, reflect, journal, and pray through Psalm 97.

Day Four

> *The soul of Jonathan was knit to the soul of David,*
> *and Jonathan loved him as his own soul.*

1 SAMUEL 18:1 NKJV

As men begin to find their identity in Christ, they become less fearful of intimacy and the barriers begin to fall. Spiritual giants tend to have close and rewarding friendships with other men.

What are some ways you could pray, here, for your husband's spiritual growth?

If you are falling deeply in love with Jesus, it will be contagious.

My wife Julie can hardly wait to get up in the morning to get out of bed to go and spend time with Jesus. It makes me jealous to have what she has. I want to go deeper in my walk as well.

—JOHN BRESTIN

Jesus, help me to fall deeper in love with You.

Read, reflect, journal, and pray through Psalm 98.

Day Five

> *However, each one of you also must love his wife as he loves himself,*
> *and the wife must respect her husband.*

*I*f a friend seems jealous of your time with your husband, or if she makes derogatory remarks about him, beware.

Do you have any women friends who are constantly putting your husband down? Do they have legitimate reasons to want you to take a stand because he is abusive? Or could jealousy be involved?

*T*here have been times when I have thought that my friend made a poor choice of a husband, but because I value the sanctity of marriage, I need to be supportive of that marriage! The only exception to this is when, because of a husband's substance abuse, physical abuse, or infidelity, you need to give your friend the support she needs to separate from him and exercise tough love, the kind of love that says, "I love you—but I will not tolerate this behavior. Therefore, we can't be together unless you get the help you need to make a genuine change." This kind of tough love is not anti-marriage, but pro-marriage, for boundaries must be set in order for the marriage to have any hope at all.

Lord, help me be a real friend to my married friends, helping them to think well of their husbands. But Lord, if a friend is in danger, then help me give her the support she needs to separate and demand that her husband get help.

Read, reflect, journal, and pray through Psalm 99.

How is it between us, Lord?

How is it between me and my sisters (or brothers)?

CAN AN EX-WIFE AND A NEW WIFE GET ALONG?

Day One

> *Wasn't it enough that you took away my husband?*
>
> GENESIS 30:15

Though Jesus elevated the status of women, and polygamy nearly disappeared, many women today face pain similar to their polygamous ancestors. If you are an ex-wife or a new wife, and if there are children involved, then you are a "wife-in-law" and how you act will affect you, your children, and your children's children.

 What kind of painful feelings do you imagine an ex-wife has? What kind of challenging situations?

I felt like Godzilla facing Venus. It was the first time I had seen them as a couple, a family. I thought I had a grip on it all, but when I went back into the house I cried for the entire night. I can't describe the loneliness, the unhappiness. I was convinced that no one would ever love me again. I felt used up, discarded, and ridiculous.

—AN ANONYMOUS EX-WIFE INTERVIEWED BY ANN CRYSTER

 Do you have friends who have felt rejected and discarded by a man? Who are they, how might you pray for them, and how might you encourage them of their value?

Lord, may I be Your love to those who have not been loved well by others.

Read, reflect, journal, and pray through Psalm 100.

Day Two

Then Rachel said, "I have had a great struggle
with my sister, and I have won."

GENESIS 30:8

The new wife's life is not necessarily a bed of roses. She may know her husband is capable of breaking his vows, and she may wonder if there are some things he misses about his first wife. Even if she was not responsible for the break-up in the marriage, she may have fears and insecurities about the solidity of the marriage, about the affection of his children for her, and about her acceptance as the "new wife" in the Christian community.

Do you have a friend who is a second wife—either because of divorce or death? In what ways is her life challenging? How could you pray for her and show her the love of Christ?

Divorce is a minefield, and you cannot walk through it without injury. Every wife-in-law has been genuinely hurt.

 What do you think are some of the reasons that God's intention for marriage was to be permanent? If you are a victim of divorce, how might you be able to comfort others, in some way, with the comfort you have received from God?

> Even though she [the new wife] has the license and the ring, she feels that the competition will never end. At the back of her mind lurks the fear that her husband still pines for his ex-wife, even more attractive now that she is forbidden fruit.
>
> —ANN CRYSTER

Lord, help me to take out the log in my own eye instead of looking for the splinter in others.

Read, reflect, journal, and pray through Psalm 101.

Day Three

Rachel envied her sister.

GENESIS 30:1 NKJV

The inability to forgive and the inability to conquer the debilitating emotions of jealousy, resentment, and bitterness are the two most common obstacles preventing a healthy relationship between wives-in-law.

 Why is forgiveness so difficult? Who do you have trouble forgiving?

I had lost my mate, and to some extent my social position. I know my wife-in-law [husband's new wife] is much better off financially than I am. She's the one taking the fancy trips and redecorating her home while I'm pinching pennies. But one thing I wasn't prepared for was my five-year-old daughter coming to me one day and saying, "Oh, Mommy, Mara makes the best fried chicken, and we had so much fun planting a garden together. I can't wait to go back next Saturday."

—INTERVIEW BY ANN CRYSTER

> Lack of forgiveness is the poison we drink hoping others will die.

*I*t is hard to forgive someone who has genuinely wronged you, especially if they are unrepentant. We cannot—absolutely cannot—do it on our own. But a prayer God is eager to answer is: *Lord, give me grace for* _____. *Give me genuine and not just outward forgiveness.* Professional biblical counseling can also be the lifeline when you are sinking in the quicksand of bitterness. We cannot get out by ourselves. We need the Spirit of God and His people to help us.

Father, please help me forgive those who have hurt me. Give me compassion, grace, and perspective.

Read, reflect, journal, and pray through Psalm 102.

Day Four

Make this your common practice: Confess your sins to each other and pray for each other so that you can live together whole and healed. The prayer of a person living right with God is something powerful to be reckoned with.

JAMES 5:16 MSG

*W*hen unforgiveness abounds, the damaging effects ripple out to the next generation.

 If there is someone you are holding a grudge against, and try as you might, you can't seem to let it go—would you consider confessing this to someone you trust? What might be the consequences if you do not?

They wouldn't attend the same family functions. Everyone had to phone around beforehand to make sure that so-and-so wasn't coming. If one showed up, the other left. My cousin's wedding was a fiasco. It made me very nervous about any sort of "family" occasion. So when I got married I didn't invite any of them, step-parents or parents, just some friends and my sister. I didn't want their stupidity to spoil my wedding.

—INTERVIEW BY GLYNNIS WALKER

*J*f a woman is able to behave in a reasonable fashion toward her wife-in-law, it impresses the children immeasurably.

They were great friends. My mother said she always liked Elaine and didn't blame her for anything. It made me respect my mother an awful lot for having such a mature attitude.

—INTERVIEW BY GLYNNIS WALKER

Father, I lift up those of my friends who have to deal with the complicated effects of divorce. Draw them closer to You during this difficult time.

Read, reflect, journal, and pray through Psalm 103.

Day Five

This time my husband will treat me with honor,
because I have borne him six sons.

GENESIS 30:20

*W*e can learn something from Leah. She eventually changed dreams. Instead of hoping for her husband's love, she hoped for his honor.

Solomon tells us there is a time to persist and a time to give up. Why is it sometimes wise to "change dreams"?

Be still before the Lord and ask Him how to stoke the fires of your perennial friendships. If He leads you to send brief e-mails, to pray, or to call—do it. Then write what you did.

Life has meaning,
even when hopes are
unfulfilled.

—LARRY RICHARDS

For years I clung unrealistically to the dream that Matt would come back. In so doing, I hurt Molly. I fed her hope of reconciliation. I did what I could to keep Molly from loving Brooke, because I was afraid if she did, it would be another nail in the coffin of my marriage to Matt. But as time went by, God helped me to see I was robbing Molly of the joy of childhood—and possibly maiming her for life.

One year, when she was just six, after she had spent Christmas with Matt and Brooke, I found her in her room in tears. She told me she hated Christmas. A six-year-old? Hating Christmas? As I drew her out, I heard her parroting my criticisms of Brooke. God convicted me that Molly was reflecting my bitterness—and out of loyalty to me, was withholding her love and cooperation.

We had a long talk that night, and I confessed to Molly that I had been wrong in not fully forgiving Brooke and her dad. That was a turning point. Her relationship with Matt and Brooke improved dramatically—and intriguingly, so did mine.

—Penny

Search me, O God, and see if there be any wicked way in me, and lead me in the paths of righteousness.

Read, reflect, journal, and pray through Psalm 104.

How is it between us, Lord?

How is it between me and my sisters (or brothers)?

RESTORING OUR SISTERS TO THEIR SENSES

Day One

> *Brothers, if someone is caught in a sin, you who are spiritual should restore him gently. But watch yourself, or you also may be tempted.*
>
> GALATIANS 6:1

A hard-line approach with Scripture verses flying tends to increase resistance. Your friend is often convinced that her choice, even if it goes against Scripture, is the only choice she can make for her happiness. The scriptural choice seems too hard and painful. Therefore, one of the most effective ways to "restore a friend to her senses" is to gently help her to see what the consequences of her choice will be.

List some of the lifelong consequences of choosing marriage to an unbeliever. Be specific.

List some of the long-term consequences of choosing abortion.

I've found that often the easier road leads to enormous regret and lifelong pain, but the harder road leads to lasting peace and joy.

—LEE EZELL,
A WOMAN WHO CHOSE LIFE

Lord, give me wisdom and gentleness in restoring sisters to their senses.

Read, reflect, journal, and pray through Psalm 105.

Day Two

Speaking the truth in love.

EPHESIANS 4:15

Truth without love is judgment. Love without truth is destructive.

 With your closest friends, how willing are you to speak the truth in love? Comment on the above statement.

When I was going through an eating disorder, I simply couldn't see what was happening with my body. But my friends could, and they kept telling me, "You've got to get help."

—KATHY TROCCOLI

*M*arriage is sacred to God. Divorce was never His intention. However, if a spouse has already broken the marriage vows through infidelity or abandonment, out of mercy, divorce is permitted—though not required. If a spouse is abusive or addicted, Scripture permits separation. There is nothing wrong with saying, "I love you. You have to get help. I am separating from you until you get help and there is the fruit of genuine change in your life." Often this tough love is the only hope for a marriage.

What are some of the consequences of not separating from an abusive or addicted spouse?

Lord, give me Your wisdom when I talk to friends. Give me Your humility when they talk to me.

Read, reflect, journal, and pray through Psalm 106.

Day Three

Wounds from a friend can be trusted,
but an enemy multiplies kisses.

PROVERBS 27:6

Often it is acquaintances who confront and close friends who stay mum, when it should be the other way around. We are more likely to trust the "wounds of a friend."

Think about the times when you have been confronted and responded to the confrontation with a teachable heart. What do you remember about the confrontation and why do you think you were able to hear?

I felt like life was passing me by. I began to be irritated by all kinds of little things about my husband. He was too skinny. I thought he had ugly fingers. He was a farmer and sometimes he had dirt in his ears. I know it sounds ridiculous, but at the time I felt that if there was going to be any hope for happiness for me, I had to leave. A few years after the divorce, though, I thought, *What was the matter with me? He was a good man!* During that time of brokenness I came to Christ. But though He made me a new creation, and filled the emptiness in me, that doesn't mean I escaped the consequences of my sinful choice.

—BETH, A WOMAN FROM NEW MEXICO

What are some ways a true friend might effectively help us see our blind spots?

*J*can't go willy-nilly pointing out faults. I must choose carefully or my friend will stop listening. But when I see her headed down a destructive path, what kind of friend am I if I stay silent?

Lord, when friends speak hard things to me,
make me teachable.

Read, reflect, journal, and pray through Psalm 107.

Day Four

A prudent man sees danger and takes refuge,
but the simple keep going and suffer for it.

PROVERBS 22:3

*H*elping one another see and respond to danger, whether it is the consequences of neglecting to discipline children or neglecting to love your husband, is part of our high calling as sisters in Christ.

   Do you have sisters who are willing to speak the truth to you about dangers you may be choosing? If not, what could you do?

*S*ometimes there are big choices, such as divorce or sexual immorality, with severe repercussions; other times the choices may not *seem* so significant, but indeed, are. The habit of choosing gossip, gluttony, or constant television can be like pouring water that is continually quenching the flame of God's Spirit.

   Do you and your friends speak the truth to one another regularly so you can go higher? If not, what could you do?

I never realized how hard choosing divorce would make my life. Family traditions, like carving pumpkins and putting up the Christmas tree, are changed. The kids are always thinking of the missing parent. We all dread the holidays. The kids aren't eager to be with me or my ex-husband. They aren't particularly comfortable with our new spouses. Home isn't home. There's constant friction concerning where they'll go, and when they come it's painful—because it isn't the same for them. It isn't the same for me either. I can't turn to David and say, "Do you remember the Christmas when Johnny ..." because David wasn't there. And special occasions, like birthdays, graduations, weddings, etc., are all filled with distress. The pain won't quit—and often, it's terribly intense.

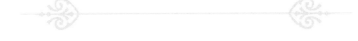

May I not be deceived by my own foolish heart, O Lord.

Read, reflect, journal, and pray through Psalm 108.

Day Five

Do not rebuke a mocker or he will hate you;
rebuke a wise man and he will love you.

PROVERBS 9:8

*J*f we agree with Scripture that our depravity is real, we should stretch toward honesty in our communication with one another. Not only should we speak the truth, we absolutely must receive the truth with humble hearts.

What are some of the times you remember that a friend had the courage to speak the truth to you, you received it, and it made a difference in your life?

_____

_____

_____

_____

_____

_____

_____

_____

_____

_____

_____

_____

_____

_____

_____

_____

_____

_____

_____

_____

_____

_____

I so appreciate friends with teachable hearts—who listen with hearing ears, who don't become defensive. My dear friend Jill, who is as pure a heart as I know, will get tears in her eyes and say, "What you say, Dee, is true—and I receive it—thank you for speaking the truth to me." This is why Jill keeps going higher.

How well do you receive criticism?

Until the day breaks and the shadows flee,
I will go to the mountain of myrrh.

SONG OF SONGS 4:6

Lord, help me remember that to die to myself leads to life. Give me a teachable heart.

Read, reflect, journal, and pray through Psalm 109.

How is it between us, Lord?

How is it between me and my sisters (or brothers)?

SISTERS: WALKING THIS ROAD TOGETHER

Day One

> *Do not forsake your friend and the friend of your father, and do not go to your brother's house when disaster strikes you—better a neighbor nearby than a brother far away.*

Asking for help, rather than being a sign of weakness, is a sign of strength because it demonstrates humility, the recognition that there are times in my life when I need help to carry an overburden. And if the need is genuine, rather than straining a friendship, asking for help cements it.

> Describe a time when you asked for help and the response was wonderful. What do you remember about it?

*W*hen it was clear Steve *was* dying, and I had retreats I simply couldn't do, Liz Curtis Higgs was willing to break her precious sabbatical. She said, "I'll go at the drop of a hat, Dee. And I'll send the honorarium to you." How could I *not* love a woman like that? That kind of response *cements* a friendship.

How have you really been there for friends when they needed you the most? What have you learned from this?

May I respond to my friends' needs before
they have to ask.

Read, reflect, journal, and pray through Psalm 110.

Day Two

*Carry each other's burdens, and in this way you
will fulfill the law of Christ.*

GALATIANS 6:2

*S*hell's enthusiastic response, her absolute *eagerness* to help me,
lifted the burden from my shoulders. Had she said, "Well, if you
can't find someone else ..." I would have retreated. I might even have
felt "let down," despite the fact I had minimized my need, which was,
in fact, great.

Why is it so hard to ask for help—even when our need is
great? What should this teach us when others ask for help?

The Greek word for burden in Galatians 6:2 means "over-burden." Later, when we are told each man should carry his own load, the word is "an everyday load."

 Describe "everyday" loads in your life for which you should not ask for help. Then, describe some "over-burdens" you have faced.

Lord, help me always carry my own load, but to ask for help when I have an "over-burden."

Read, reflect, journal, and pray through Psalm 111.

Day Three

Perfume and incense bring joy to the heart,
and the pleasantness of one's friend springs from his earnest counsel.

PROVERBS 27:9

Earnest counsel is so different from advice off the top of your head! My friend Shell prayed over my decision, sought God's face, and then wrote me a ten-page letter filled with Scripture verses that she thought might help me discern God's will.

What friends are likely to give you earnest counsel? Can you remember a time when it was particularly helpful? Why?

*Lord, help me be an active listener, drawing out
the deep waters of another's soul.*

Read, reflect, journal, and pray through Psalm 112.

Day Four

The purposes of a man's heart are deep waters,
but a man of understanding draws them out.

Proverbs 20:5

*J*eremiah tells us we have deceitful hearts. I didn't even know why I didn't want to adopt this little girl—and I could have given some pretty spiritual reasons. But my friend Sara kept asking me questions until we both saw that my reasons were selfish, prideful, and wrong.

🏵 Describe a friend who is a particularly good example of the above proverb—because of the way she listens. What can you learn from her?

Are there some areas in your life where you are stuck? You've tried to change—but can't? Is there a sister in Christ who might help you see your blind spots?

Lord, give me wisdom on who might be able to draw out the deep waters of my soul, on who might free me when I am bogged down and stuck.

Read, reflect, journal, and pray through Psalm 113.

Day Five

Two people can accomplish more than twice as much as one;
they get a better return for their labor. If one person falls, the other can reach
out and help. But people who are alone when they fall are in real trouble.

ECCLESIASTES 4:9–10 NLT

Spend some time in thanksgiving for your sisters who have
exemplified the above passage.

Spend some time evaluating how well you love. Evaluate how well you listen, how well you speak the truth, how well you fill up their souls with edifying thoughts, how well you respond to their needs, and how well you give grace.

Father, may we, as your children, live together like one big happy family, full of sympathy toward each other and loving one another with tender hearts and humble minds. And may You give us Your blessing as we pray for each other and help each other in any way we can. I ask all this in the power and grace of Your only begotten Son, Jesus Christ.

Read, reflect, journal, and pray through Psalm 114.

How is it between us, Lord?

How is it between me and my sisters (or brothers)?

*Additional copies of this and
other Honor products are available
wherever good books are sold.*

If you have enjoyed this book,
or if it has had an impact on your life,
we would like to hear from you.

Please contact us at:

Honor Books
Cook Communications Ministries, Dept. 201
4050 Lee Vance View
Colorado Springs, CO 80918
Or visit our Web site:
www.cookministries.com